ALL ABOUT...

THE

Tudors

HEATHER MORRIS

HODDER
Wayland

an imprint of Hodder Children's Books

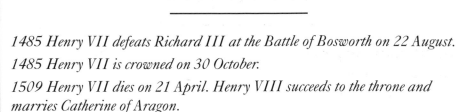

TIMELINE

1485 Henry VII defeats Richard III at the Battle of Bosworth on 22 August.

1485 Henry VII is crowned on 30 October.

1509 Henry VII dies on 21 April. Henry VIII succeeds to the throne and marries Catherine of Aragon.

1513 Invading Scots are defeated at the Battle of Flodden Field on 9 September.

1526–29 Henry VIII negotiates with the Pope about divorcing Catherine.

1533 Henry VIII marries Anne Boleyn in secret and Elizabeth is born.

1534 Henry VIII becomes Supreme Head of the Church of England.

1535 Sir Thomas More is beheaded on 6 July.

1536–1539 Dissolution of the Monasteries.

1547 Henry VIII dies and Edward VI succeeds.

1553 Edward VI dies, Lady Jane Grey becomes queen for nine days, then Mary Tudor succeeds.

1556 Archbishop Thomas Cranmer is burnt at the stake.

1558 Calais is captured by the French. Mary dies on 17 November and Elizabeth becomes Queen.

1568 Mary Queen of Scots arrives in England.

1578 Francis Drake starts on his voyage round the world in the Golden Hind. *He arrives back in 1580.*

1587 Mary Queen of Scots is executed at Fotheringhay Castle.

1587 Sir Walter Raleigh lands in Virginia.

1588 The Spanish Armada is defeated.

1592 First of Shakespeare's plays is performed.

1601 Earl of Essex is executed for attempted rebellion.

1603 Elizabeth I dies on 24 March and is succeeded by James VI of Scotland.

CONTENTS

THE FIRST TUDOR KING

F or nearly fifty years two powerful families, the Yorks and the Lancasters, fought over the English throne in the Wars of the Roses. On 22 August 1485, Henry Tudor defeated Richard III, the last Yorkist king, at the Battle of Bosworth. He was crowned Henry VII on

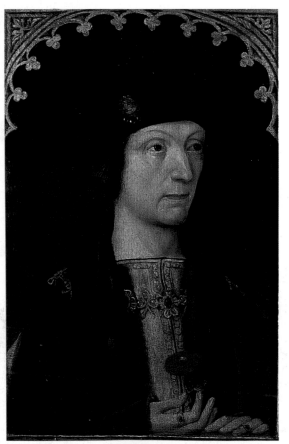

30 October in Westminster Abbey. In the following year Henry married Elizabeth of York to bring peace between the families.

Henry VII claimed that he was an ancestor of King Arthur.

She had eight children, but only three survived. Although his claim to the throne was weak, Henry was a cautious and clever king who brought peace and stability to the country. He strengthened the government and laid a strong foundation for the Tudor dynasty. He was only 52 when he died.

Henry built several royal chapels and palaces, including Richmond Palace on the River Thames. He died there on 21 April 1509.

HENRY VIII

Henry VIII became king when he was only 18 years old. He was very different from his father. He was well educated, and wrote poetry and music. He was also a good archer, and loved tournaments, tennis and hunting. Once when he was hawking, he pole-vaulted over a stream, the pole broke, he became stuck head-first in the mud and nearly died.

A diplomat described Henry as 'above the usual height, with an extremely fine calf to his leg, his complexion very fair and bright, auburn hair combed straight and short.'

Henry loved extravagant display and when he met the king of France at the Field of the Cloth of Gold there were fountains flowing with real wine.

Although popular, Henry was a much less careful king than his father had been and during his reign money was a constant problem. He spent a lot of money on his army and navy and fought wars with France and Scotland. King James IV of Scotland was killed in the battle of Flodden Field in 1513 but Henry never managed to defeat France or Scotland. He brought Wales under the control of English laws and parliament, although most of its people continued to speak Welsh.

HENRY VIII'S WIVES

Marriage, and having a male heir, was important for the Tudors. Henry's first wife, Catherine of Aragon, had six children but only Mary survived. Henry still hoped for a son and had met Anne Boleyn whom he wanted to marry. To marry Anne, he divorced Catherine but Anne's only child was Elizabeth. To marry again, Henry had Anne executed. Next, Henry married Jane Seymour who finally produced a son, Edward.

After twenty-four years of marriage, Catherine did not want a divorce but Henry made Parliament agree to it.

Henry married Anne Boleyn in secret but soon grew tired of her. At Hampton Court the initials HA, for Henry and Anne, were being painted over as she was executed.

Jane died soon after the birth of Edward. Henry's fourth wife was a German princess, Anne of Cleves. They married reluctantly and Anne soon agreed to a divorce. Just sixteen days later, Henry married Catherine Howard who was only nineteen. Like her cousin Anne, Catherine was executed. By now Henry was old and sick and his final wife, Katherine Parr, nursed him until he died.

Henry had never met Anne of Cleves before their marriage, but had seen a flattering portrait which left out her smallpox scars.

THE ENGLISH REFORMATION

R eligious change swept through Europe in the sixteenth century with many people rejecting the Catholic Church which had become greedy and corrupt. These people became known as Protestants.

Archbishop Thomas Cranmer who translated the Prayer Book into English in 1549. He was burnt at the stake by Mary I.

When Mary I became Queen, many Protestants were burnt for refusing to return to the Catholic Church.

It was Henry VIII's wish to divorce Catherine of Aragon that made him defy the Pope and declare himself head of the Church of England. Some Catholics refused to accept this and were executed, including Sir Thomas More who had been Lord Chancellor. For ordinary people, the most obvious change was that the Prayer Book and Bible were translated into English for the first time, although servants, labourers and women were forbidden to read them. Monasteries and abbeys were also destroyed and most of the monks and friars became parish priests. Their wealth and lands were taken by Henry and sold.

Lacock Abbey was the last abbey to be converted into a private house, in 1539.

EDWARD VI

Edward was a sickly child of nine when he became king and he died only six years later. Lord Northumberland tried to make his Protestant daughter-in-law, Lady Jane Grey, queen although she had no real right to the throne. Henry's eldest daughter Mary was proclaimed queen instead and Jane was executed. She was only 16 years old and was queen for just nine days.

Edward was the son of Jane Seymour, Henry VIII's favourite wife. He was never strong and died of tuberculosis in 1553.

MARY I

Mary was the daughter of Catherine of Aragon and was also a dedicated Catholic. She felt great resentment about the way her mother had been treated and tried to reverse many of Henry's religious changes. Over 300 Protestants were burnt during her reign, mostly ordinary people, but also five bishops including Archbishop Thomas Cranmer. Mary was already 38 when she married and she had no children. She died in 1558 from influenza.

Mary married the Catholic King Philip of Spain in 1554. Their marriage was unpopular with the people.

ELIZABETH I

Elizabeth was Mary's half sister. She was 25 years old when she became queen. Elizabeth was clever, learned, spoke five languages and loved hunting, dancing and music. She had also experienced many troubles, including her mother's execution and the country's religious unrest. In her first speech to Parliament, she declared: 'I thank God I am endued with such qualities that if I were turned out of the realm in my petticoat, I were able to live in any place in Christendom.'

Elizabeth had many formal portraits painted showing her in robes of state to emphasize her right to the throne.

16

Despite having many suitors, Elizabeth never married, preferring to govern on her own. Under her rule the country became peaceful and prosperous. She died in 1603, aged 69, and named James VI of Scotland, the son of Mary Queen of Scots, as her heir. Elizabeth was the last Tudor monarch.

Elizabeth went on long, magnificent journeys round the country so ordinary people could see her. In Kent, a banquet with 140 dishes was cooked for her.

THE ARMADA

I n July 1588 the Spanish launched a great Armada to invade England and restore a Catholic to the throne. They sent 130 ships with 2,400 guns and 30,000 men, mainly soldiers. Elizabeth I ordered her fleet to attack. There were about 140 vessels in the English fleet, both warships and privately owned ships, and 10,000 men. The British ships were easier to manoeuvre than the Spanish vessels and were sailed by expert seamen.

This design for a tapestry of the Armada shows the Spanish galleons driven by oars.

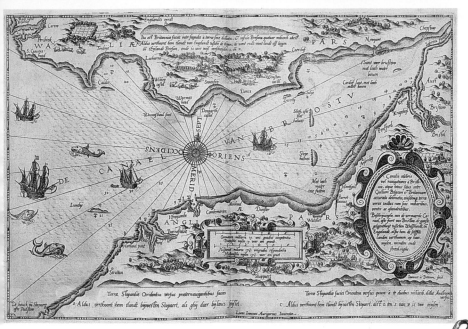

A map of the route of the Armada, showing the Bristol Channel.

The English attacked the Spanish fleet off Calais with guns and fireships and prevented them from landing. Finally, gales blew the Spanish ships north round Scotland and Ireland and most were wrecked. Only half the Spanish fleet returned home. The victory medal was inscribed 'God blew and they were scattered.'

Treasure from the wrecked Spanish ships was washed up in Ireland.

19

How the Country Was Ruled

In Tudor times Parliament did not meet often and was not elected by the people. The monarch needed Parliament mainly to raise money from taxes, especially for fighting wars. There was no general income tax and Tudor monarchs were always quite poor. Under Henry VII Parliament hardly met. Henry VIII was not interested at first, but then he used Parliament to get his divorce from Catherine. Elizabeth I took almost all important decisions herself, although she did need Parliament to pass some laws and to raise money from taxation. However, she also criticised Parliament for interfering in other matters 'beyond the reach of a subject's brain'.

Elizabeth in her Parliament robes in 1559.

Elizabeth I and Parliament. Many official Parliamentary posts like those of the Speaker and Black Rod exist today.

Order was kept in towns and the country by unpaid Sheriffs and Justices of the Peace. As well as holding trials they were responsible for maintaining roads and bridges, looking after the poor, and controlling wages, prices and ale-houses. Criminals and the poor were often flogged or hanged for minor offences as there was a general fear of unrest and rebellion.

Punishments were often harsh – here two fake fortune tellers are in the pillory.

TOWN AND COUNTRYSIDE

T owns in Tudor England grew rapidly. The
population of London was about four times bigger
in 1600 than in 1500, at 200,000. The cities of Bristol,
York and Norwich had populations of more than 20,000.
There were many fine new buildings but conditions
were still cramped and dirty with no proper drainage.
Plague and diseases often swept through crowded
towns, but they remained lively places where many
different tradespeople worked and enjoyed the taverns
and theatres.

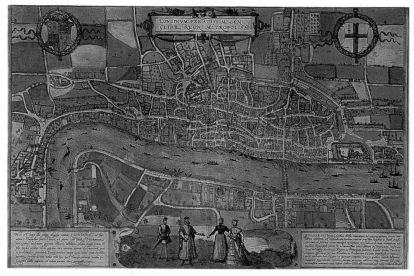

*Tudor London showing the Tower of London on the edge of the city
to the right and fields south of the River Thames.*

Country life was hard with no machines to help with the back-breaking work.

Villagers grew their own food. They also looked after livestock and kept bees for honey. The growth of towns made trade possible too. Counties around London supplied food and drink to markets like Smithfield (meat) and Covent Garden (fruit and vegetables). There were improvements in farming with the introduction of new crops like maize, hops and potatoes.

Wealthy Tudors often built beautiful gardens on their country estates. Formal designs called knot gardens with paths, clipped trees and hedges separating beds of plants were popular.

PEOPLE'S JOBS

The cloth trade was very important. Wool weaving skills had been brought to England by refugees and whole families still worked on looms in their own houses. There were some factories as this ballad describes, 'Within one room being large and long, There stood two hundred looms full strong.' Wool and finished cloth were transported by pack horses and exported round Europe and to new colonies in the East and West Indies and America. Sea and river ports became busy.

Carpenters at work. New building projects meant there was plenty of work for skilled tradesmen.

In the north of England, mines were opened because coal was replacing wood as the main fuel. Deep sea fishing, especially for herring, supplemented scarce meat supplies. More people learned to read and write and worked in administration because the Dissolution of the Monasteries meant that the Church no longer provided educated clerks for these jobs.

A workman's felt hat, and shears for cutting cloth. East Anglia, Yorkshire and the Cotswolds were centres of the wool trade.

25

LIFE AT HOME

The design of grand houses changed as they were divided into separate rooms rather than the single large hall of medieval times. Brick began to be used instead of stone. Inside, the ceilings and walls were richly decorated with painted panels, plasterwork and tapestries. Floors were of brick, tiles or rush matting. People did have carpets, but often hung them on walls. When Henry VIII died he owned sixty 'great carpets'.

Burghley House was enlarged by William Cecil, one of Elizabeth's favourite ministers. It features large windows which became popular among the rich as more glass was imported.

Even rich people did not have much furniture and clothes were stored in chests.

Richer people sat at tables on chairs at mealtimes but paintings also show them sitting on the floor on cushions.

For the poor, life was much simpler and harder. Houses were built from timber with clay and rubble filling the gaps. The floors were trodden earth and they had only basic furniture made by local craftsmen. Bad harvests meant real starvation for many. Unemployed farm workers or soldiers returned from war often became beggars.

A nobleman passing a beggar. Local parishes had to provide employment and relief for the poor.

BEING A CHILD

More schools were set up by wealthy individuals but most children were not able to go to them. School had to be paid for and many children couldn't attend because their families needed them to work. For boys, reading was becoming important, both for work and to read and study the Bible.

A master and his pupils with geometrical instruments, slates and books.

Hornbooks were used to practise reading.

School days were long, starting at six in the morning, and pupils were often beaten.

Wealthy girls were educated at home by tutors and many, such as Elizabeth I, Lady Jane Grey and Sir Thomas More's daughter Margaret Roper, became good scholars. Others attended school and increasing numbers learned to read, although not necessarily to write. Some girls were sent away to another household to become waiting gentlewomen. All children were expected to show great respect to their parents, to stand in front of them and call them Sir and Madam.

TUDOR WOMEN

omen in Tudor England had more freedom than many other women in Europe. In 1590, a German wrote, 'they often stroll out or drive by coach in very gorgeous clothes, and the men must put up with such ways.' Women were expected to get married and the rich often married very young. Henry VII's mother was only thirteen when he was born.

Lord Cobham and his family. Most married women had between eight and fifteen children but usually only half survived to adulthood.

Country women worked hard – milking, making cheese and butter, raising poultry and growing vegetables. They also made rush lights, tallow candles and soap. Wool was spun and woven at home, and bread had to be baked, beer brewed and food cooked and preserved for winter. In towns, women could be tailors, milliners, or embroiderers. They also kept inns, did laundry and sold fish. Some trade guilds were open to women.

The farmer's wife looked after the poultry and the dairy and took butter, cheese, eggs and chickens to market. She kept the money she earned.

31

WHAT PEOPLE ATE

Food in Tudor times was less varied than today, and it changed with the seasons as it was hard to keep fresh. Bread was a basic food for everyone. In his journals, the traveller Fynes Moryson wrote: 'husbandmen eat barley and rye brown bread; but citizens and gentlemen eat most pure white bread.'

A kitchen in a wealthy household. The rich enjoyed banquets with many courses.

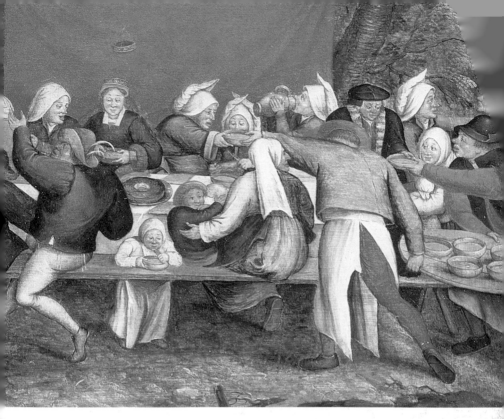

The Wedding Feast, *by Pieter Brueghel, shows poor people eating soup and bread off wooden and pewter plates. Everyone, even children, drank weak beer because the water was unsafe to drink.*

Meat included beef, mutton, bacon, chicken, goose, duck and game such as venison and rabbit. It was compulsory to eat fish during Lent and on Fridays. There were cabbages and onions but not many other vegetables. Fruit and nuts were popular. Towards the end of the period new foods began to arrive from the Americas such as potatoes, tomatoes, peppers, maize and turkeys. Forks were not used and even the rich ate with knives, spoons and fingers.

What People Wore

For everyone, clothes were quite valuable and were looked after carefully. They were often passed on after death. John Warden, a yeoman from Essex, gave his shirts, doublet, breeches and jerkin to his friends in his will. Henry VIII owned thirty-three linen shirts when he died.

A man's richly embroidered cloak, hat and gloves. Tudor men also adorned themselves with earrings.

This marriage scene shows a variety of people – the better dressed are on the left while the dancers wear more ordinary clothes.

For the fashion-conscious rich, clothes were very expensive. A single gown could cost more than the average person earned in a year. What people were allowed to wear was also regulated. For example, only knights could wear leopard fur. Dyeing was expensive so strong colours, especially black and red, were a sign of wealth. Poorer people wore undyed clothes of brown or white. Children wore small versions of grown-up clothes.

BOOKS AND THEATRE

Printed books, produced on presses developed by William Caxton, were becoming more widely available but were still expensive. They were also considered dangerous and the only presses allowed were in London and at Oxford and Cambridge universities. Most of the books published were on serious subjects like religion, science, mathematics and poetry. Writing poetry was an important social skill and some of the best-known poets of the time were courtiers like Sir Philip Sidney and Sir Walter Raleigh.

A ballad singer and seller. Ballads were a popular way of spreading news and political or religious arguments in Tudor times.

The theatre was popular with all classes and tickets to stand were cheap. But the theatre was treated with great suspicion by the authorities and they imposed strict rules. Women were not allowed to appear on stage, so boy apprentices played the female roles.

William Shakespeare (above) was the most important dramatist and his plays were staged at the Globe Theatre in London.

ART AND MUSIC

Many painters from Europe settled in England, including Hans Holbein who painted several portraits of Henry VIII. Tudor monarchs, especially Elizabeth, used portraits to emphasize their power and status. Her portraits often included symbols, such as her standing on a map of England to demonstrate her control over the country. Portraits were also popular among the rich and always showed them in their best clothes. Music was widespread throughout the country. Whether a person was rich or poor, it was considered an important skill to be able to play an instrument.

A miniature painted by Nicholas Hilliard. The original is only 135mm high.

Musicians playing at Wadley House. Printed sheet music was available but was very expensive.

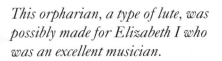

This orpharian, a type of lute, was possibly made for Elizabeth I who was an excellent musician.

MEDICINE AND HEALTH

M edicine was still based on the ancient belief that the body was governed by four elements – earth, air, fire and water. Treatments were intended to bring these into balance. Blood-letting using leeches was popular as people believed too much blood caused fevers.

Medicine gradually became more scientific. Henry VIII granted the Royal College of Surgeons four dead bodies a year from the gallows to dissect and study.

Amputations were carried out without any anaesthetic except alcohol and the wounds were not sterilized so most patients died.

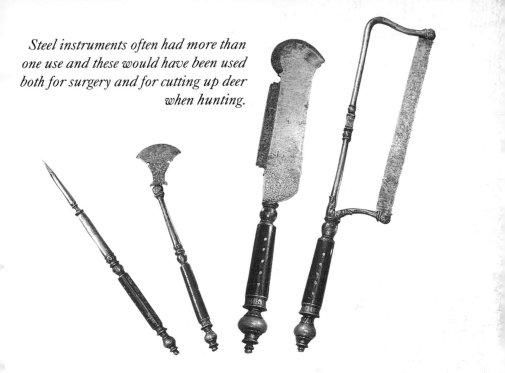

Steel instruments often had more than one use and these would have been used both for surgery and for cutting up deer when hunting.

Infectious diseases, including measles, smallpox, cholera and the plague, killed thousands, especially among the poor living in crowded and dirty conditions. Anyone could call themselves a physician and although some doctors used effective remedies there were many quacks and dangerous treatments.

A medicine chest holding 126 bottles and pots for drugs.

41

GAMES AND ENTERTAINMENTS

Public holidays were often linked to religious festivals although many were banned after the Reformation as they had become too rowdy. Often plays and pageants were part of the celebrations. The most famous festivals were held at Coventry, Chester and York. Both rich and poor enjoyed cock fights, and bear and bull baiting. Tennis and bowling were also popular. Some sports had a more serious side and in 1511 it became compulsory for all men and boys over seven to own a bow and arrows to practise archery.

This embroidered table carpet shows men hunting with hounds. Hunting was a favourite sport among the rich and also provided valuable food.

Cards were popular, as well as board games. A chess board was found on the warship Mary Rose.

Football was popular among the poor, but illegal. There were no rules and no limit to the number of players on each team. It was described as a game of 'beastly fury and extreme violence' and many people were hurt, or even killed, during games.

Peasants dancing at a wedding painted by Pieter Brueghel. Dancing was a good way of meeting the opposite sex for both rich and poor.

DISCOVERIES

Europeans' knowledge of the world changed as explorers, in tiny ships with no maps, discovered new oceans and continents. In 1492, Genoese explorer Christopher Columbus made his first voyage to America.

In 1580 Sir Francis Drake became the first Englishman to sail around the world.

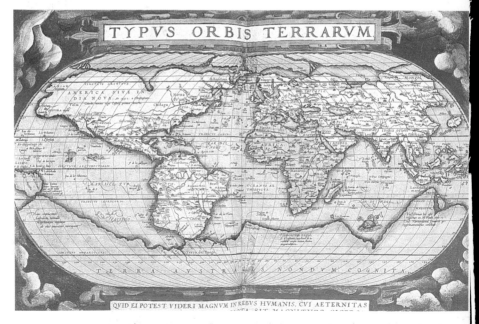

TYPVS ORBIS TERRARVM

In his ship, Golden Hind, *Drake followed the same route that Portuguese explorer Ferdinand Magellan had taken in 1522.*

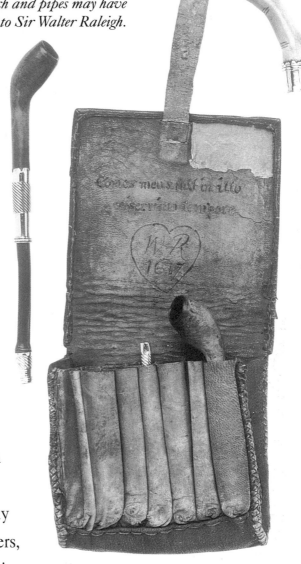

Tobacco was one of the new products brought back from the Americas. This pouch and pipes may have belonged to Sir Walter Raleigh.

English explorers, too, set out to find new routes for trade and new lands to settle. The overland trade route to India through the Middle East had become difficult and in 1587 Martin Frobisher, discovered a sea route through the far north-west of Canada. In the same year Sir Walter Raleigh tried to establish the first plantation in Virginia in America. Many sea captains were explorers, traders and pirates attacking Spanish ships and settlements. Sir John Hawkins, Treasurer to the navy, was also involved in the early days of the slave trade between Africa and America.

GLOSSARY

apprentice *A boy sent to learn a trade by living and working with a master, usually for seven years.*

Black Rod *An officer of Parliament who traditionally carried a black rod.*

breeches *Trousers, usually short ones which finish above the knee.*

Dissolution *To dissolve or get rid of something, used to describe Henry VIII's closure of the monasteries.*

doublet *A tight-fitting jacket.*

dynasty *A series of monarchs belonging to the same family.*

endued with *Given, as in 'I am given such qualities'.*

fireships *Old boats which were filled with wood, even gunpowder, set alight and sent to drift into enemy ships to set them on fire.*

galleons *Large sailing ships.*

gallows *The place where criminals were hanged.*

Guilds *An organized group of people belonging to the same trade.*

husbandmen *Farmers.*

jerkin *A short sleeveless jacket.*

Justice of the Peace or JP *A local gentleman appointed by the monarch to keep the peace.*

medieval or Middle Ages *Used to describe the period which ended with the death of Richard III.*

milliner *Someone who makes hats for a living.*

pewter *A cheap metal made from tin and lead, used for plates and cups.*

pillory *A wooden frame which locks around a person's head and hands and forces them to stand, usually in a public place.*

Protestants *Christians who split from the Catholic Church in the sixteenth century.*

quack *An unqualified doctor.*

Reformation *The movement to reform the Church.*

Sheriff *An official appointed by the monarch.*

Speaker *A member of the House of Commons elected to keep order.*

tallow *Animal fat used to make candles.*

testoon *A name for a shilling.*

tuberculosis *A disease of the lungs which was often fatal.*

venison *Meat from deer.*

yeoman *A man who owns and farms a small estate.*

INDEX